EBOOK TRAINING MANUAL

Maryanne Amadi

KDP

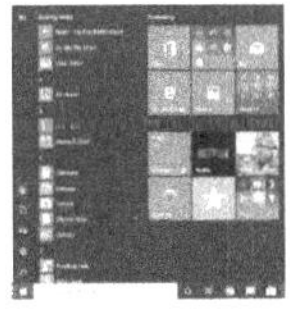

ISBN-13: 9798722230348

Cover design by: Author
Library of Congress Control Number: 2018675309
Printed in the United States of America

*This book is dedicated to God Almighty, My Parents,
My Brother, My Sisters In-laws and My Niece.*

CONTENTS

INTRODUCTION

This book will give a quick and fast way in registering, creating of kindle direct publishing (KDP) account on amazon, and how it can be use in publishing your books on amazon (eBook).

UNDERSTANDING YOUR KDP ACCOUNT*
Navigation through your account the Basic process through the book publishing using on-hands videos, that would take you into your Kdp account, is our starting point.
YOUR KDP ACCOUNT IS THE MOST IMPORTANT ELEMENT IN THE PUBLISHING BUSINESS
1. You would be expected to create or continue with your kdp.amazon.com account. I expect all here to have created theirs. If not I'd share a video to guide you on that. And please do it immediately. Don't postpone it.
2. After creation of your account I'd take you through your account, an overview
3. I'd show you how to publish your eBook & paperback the basic way, just an overview because you wouldn't need it again after this class
4. I'd next show you how to create your eBook and paperback covers respectively
5. Next I will introduce you to sense and essence of this training - USING THE KINDLE CREATE APP/SOFTWARE to format your manuscripts

CHAPTER ONE

STRONG WRITING

I t is said that a book is strong when it is compelling to read. It is a strong that is draw attention of the readers to finish.
A book or Article is strong when it impact the readers life and when the journey of the book or article us positive.

Writing a Strong Book

Writing means to scribble down something.

Writing a strong book is to meet the needs of your target audience, to the extent that they will be willing to pay for your work through KDP anything to get your work.

CHAPTER TWO

PURPOSE OF WRITING

Trust me, they are not best sellers because they wrote well but, rather because they sold well. Truth be said there are so many strong writings around but lying fallow. It's because such writers only wrote to satisfy their personalities and they wrote out of zeal but not out of need. Therefore this makes up a best seller.

HOW DO YOU KNOW WHEN TO STOP WRITING?

-When your writing becomes a struggle.

-When you feel you need to increase the volume.

-When you want to add everything and anything new or trending that you have heard

CHAPTER THREE

BEST SELLERS

A best seller is said to be a writer/publisher who has achieve financial breakthrough in the quest of writing and selling. A bestseller, is an author who wrote a book that has sold well than the rest of its kind.

This rating is within a time frame and targets sales of over 10,000 copies. Best sellers are those who can impact the readers and add value to them thereby stating the fact about the book or article.

Here are 5 tips to set your book up for success so that it has a chance of becoming a bestseller.

1. Start with a big idea.

Bestsellers are built on a big idea. Not just some old thing regurgitated in a new way. It's something fresh and interesting. Something NOVEL. You must find an idea that will get readers excited to pick up your book. This goes for fiction, nonfiction, how-to, manuscripts and memoir.

A small idea for a book results in small sales. And a book idea, well, you get the picture. J.R.R. Tolkien spent years developing the languages upon which his entire world would later be built. Don't neglect the importance of nailing a big idea before you begin writing. And don't rush the research. Follow the process!!!!

2. Write with the audience in mind. Bestsellers are sticky.

The book needs to be written in a way where it can be easily shared and talked about, because it touches on some universal theme. In other words, don't just write a book for yourself. Stephen King says you write the first draft with the door closed and the second draft with the door open. That's good protocol. I suggest you get your book written well and quickly, while weaving your big idea throughout the book.

3. Edit for clarity, not perfection. Bestsellers are clear. Take out all the clutter that distracts your reader from the true message. Editing is not about making the book grammatically perfect (if that were true, books would be typo free). Rather, it is the process of making your book into what it's supposed to be. So every time you edit your work, ask yourself, "Is this helping what I'm trying to say, or hurting it?"

4. Package your book to spread. Bestsellers are packaged to sell. The title, cover, and design are all optimized to help the message spread. The way people experience your book will affect how well the book sells and how far it spreads. Your goal is to not only get this thing into people's hands; it's to give them something they want to share. This includes the decisions you make regarding title, cover, artwork, and design etc.

5. Launching is key: Never stop launching. Bestsellers are perennial. The bestselling books of all time typically didn't come out of the gates as immediate successes. But because of their timeless nature, they just kept selling. Book launches are great, but you're going to need more than one big event to sell this thing. Understanding the three unique launch phases of a book will help you sell your first 1000 or so copies, but it won't help you sell your next 10,000 or 100,000 copies. The best way to do that is to never stop launching. You just have to keep talking about it for a long time.

CHAPTER FOUR

INTRODUCTION TO EBOOK

What do we mean is an eBook?

An eBook is a book publication in an electronic form An eBook is an electronic book, also known as an e-book or eBook, is a book publication made available in digital form, consisting of text, images, or both, readable on the flat-panel display of computers or other electronic devices."

Sections and Segments of your book to be converted to eBook or for normal publication. For you to have a good book, all these listed below must be

1. Cover page

2. Copyright page

3. Dedication, acknowledgement,

4. Table of contents

5. Introduction

6. Body (or Chapters).

7. Back page (blurb/about the author).

We shall discuss this one after the other.

However note: that the order above isn't sacrosanct. You may alter the order from items 3 to 5.

Let us start with:

1. Cover page: that's the first thing you see of a book

2. Copyright© page

That's the protection ownership rights to the contents of the book.

Note of warning: the information written in any book in the copyright pages, tells you the extent to which you can use the contents and who to contact before usage. Copyright abuse is a great crime. It can cost you money and your freedom - imprisonment. A. If you've used anyone's work to build yours, it's important you reference the owner of the original work you've used. Once you've done that, you will not be accused of plagiarism. But if you must lift a diagram of an object for example from someone's book, you must write the Author of the book to get express permission from him or her, else you've violated the copyright law.

3. Dedication, acknowledgement, praise and/or foreword, are meant to boost reception and recognition of the book, materials used besides others.

4. Table of Contents (TOC): Is a quick guide for people to peep into a particular chapter. It comes with the chapter title and the page.

5. Introduction. It is the summary of the work to give the readers summary of what is the entire book. And so introduction will be written after our whole work.

6. Body or Chapters or interior: Here you start your story. This is where you write the content. What the book is all about.

7. Back Page (blurb/ about the Author) ABOUT THE AUTHOR is a short description about you and should be written in the third person format. Also Blurb is that short description of yourself on your book, written behind or at the back of your book. IT IS ALSO KNOWN AS *ABOUT THE AUTHOR*. Though a professional/

standard book, does not have that tittle "ABOUT THE BOOK". You just go ahead and write the description.

CHAPTER FIVE

CREATING OF AMAZON (KDP) ACCOUNT

We shall be creating our accounts today on Amazon and KDP and I want you to get ready because today is going to be mainly hands on activity. But it is advisable that you use a laptop for this exercise. This will enable you have an extended screen view as we try to create the account together. However you wish to use your phone for now if you don't have access to a laptop at the moment. Thank you

So please follow this steps diligently so that you don't make any mistakes. The creation of your KDP account is the first step to registering your presence on the Amazon, which is one of the largest e-market platform in the world. Use the following steps.

Step 1. Copy and paste the following link below into your browser or type it in your browser: Type https://kdp.amazon-.com into your browser preferably Chrome or Gozila and see the screen below

Then Click on Sign Up for the First timers.

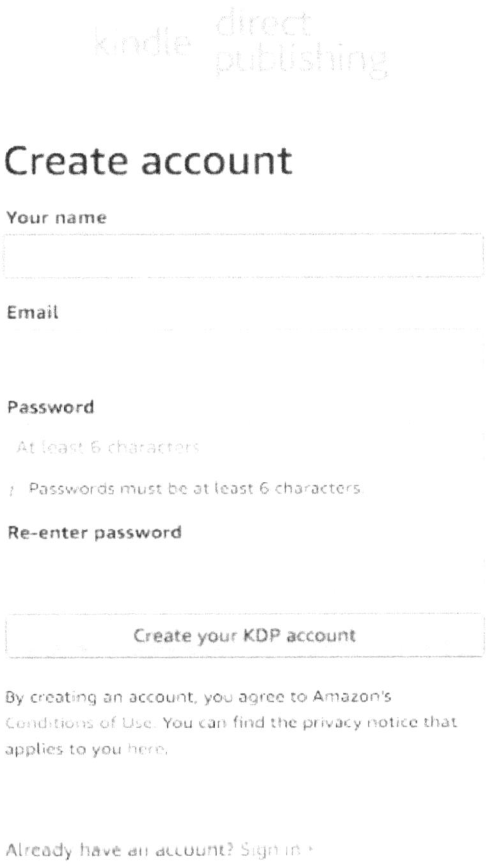
kindle direct publishing
Create account
Your name
Email
Password
At least 6 characters
Passwords must be at least 6 characters.
Re-enter password
Create your KDP account
By creating an account, you agree to Amazon's Conditions of Use. You can find the privacy notice that applies to you here.
Already have an account? Sign in

Step 2: Input all the requirement seen above and choose a password for yourself.

Check your nominated e-mail address or text message or voice message for the OTP and input it appropriately.

It's a 6-digit number, use it to fill the required space, click enter on your system and you will see the next screen�� for which I recommend that you could select "Agree" if you want to continue

Last Updated: January 4, 2021

This agreement changed on the date listed above.
See an explanation of the changes at the end of this document.

Kindle Direct Publishing Terms and Conditions

This agreement (the "Agreement") is a binding agreement between the individual or the entity identified in your Kindle Direct Publishing ("KDP") account ("you" or "Publisher") and each Amazon party. The "Amazon parties" are, individually, Amazon.com Services LLC, Amazon Media EU S.à.r.L, Amazon Services International, Inc., Amazon Serviços de Varejo do Brasil Ltda., Amazon Mexico Services, Inc., Amazon Australia Services, Inc., Amazon Asia-Pacific Holdings Private Limited, and each other Amazon affiliate that joins as a party to this Agreement. An Amazon "affiliate" is any entity that directly or indirectly controls, is controlled by, or is under common control with an Amazon party. "Amazon," "we" or "us" means, together, the Amazon parties and their affiliates.

This Agreement provides the terms and conditions of your participation in the KDP self-publication and distribution program (the "Program") and your distribution of digital content through the Program (all such content, "Digital Books") and your distribution of print content through the Program (all such content, "Print Books" and together with Digital Books, "Books"), and consists of:
• the terms set forth below;
• the Digital Pricing Page and the Print Pricing Page;
• all rules and policies for participating in the Program provided on the KDP website at http://kdp.amazon.com/ and http://kdp.amazon.co.jp/ ("Program Policies");
• the Amazon.com Conditions of Use; and
• the Amazon.com Privacy Notice.

View printer friendly version

Agree   Cancel

Please take note of the following: On the Top Panel, you will see Your Account, English, Help and Sign Out
Below: *Your Account Information is Complete*, note the statement *Create Space has moved to Kindle Direct Publishing*

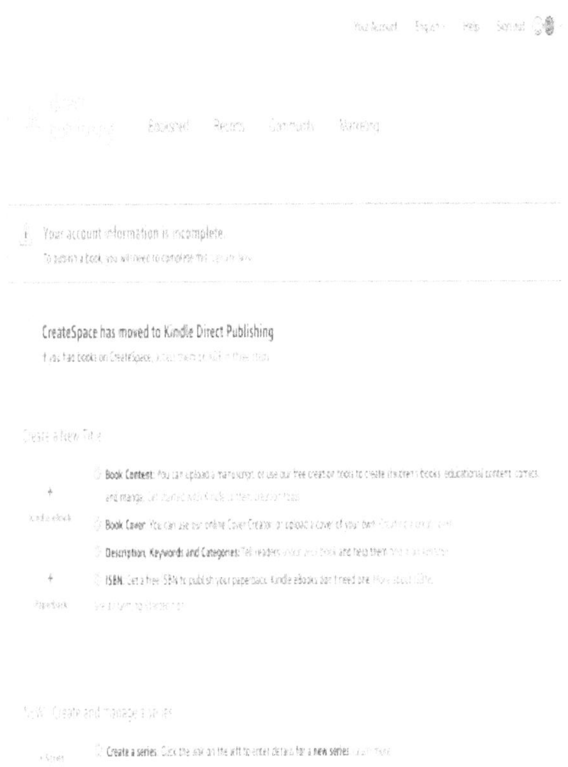

We are not done yet with the creation of account, Now click on *Your Account* and see the screen below. Draw down the US+1 code to select Nigeria or the country or your residence from the list of countries and input your phone no to recover the OTP that will be sent to you as a proof that it is yours:

Enter the OTP in the required field in the dialogue box after clicking Send OTP on the screen above and a form will be sent to you to fill��

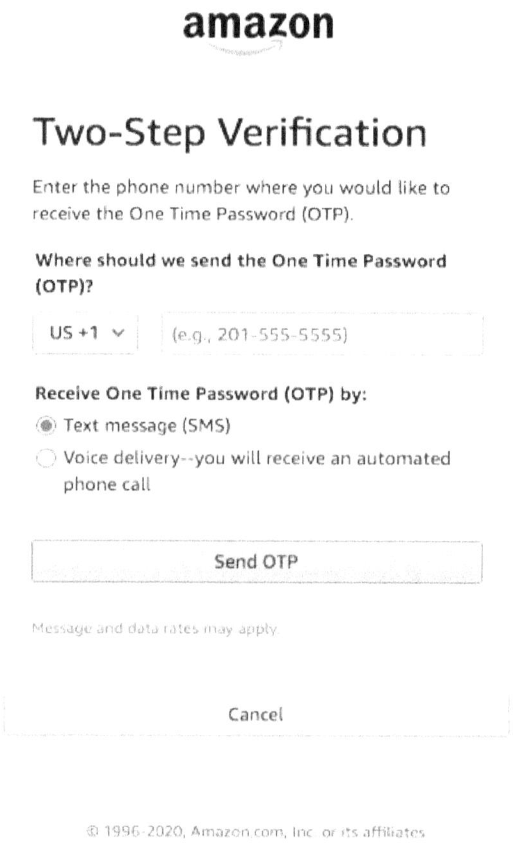

amazon

Two-Step Verification

Enter the phone number where you would like to receive the One Time Password (OTP).

Where should we send the One Time Password (OTP)?

US +1 (e.g., 201-555-5555)

Receive One Time Password (OTP) by:

- Text message (SMS)
- Voice delivery--you will receive an automated phone call

Send OTP

Message and data rates may apply.

Cancel

© 1996-2020, Amazon.com, Inc. or its affiliates

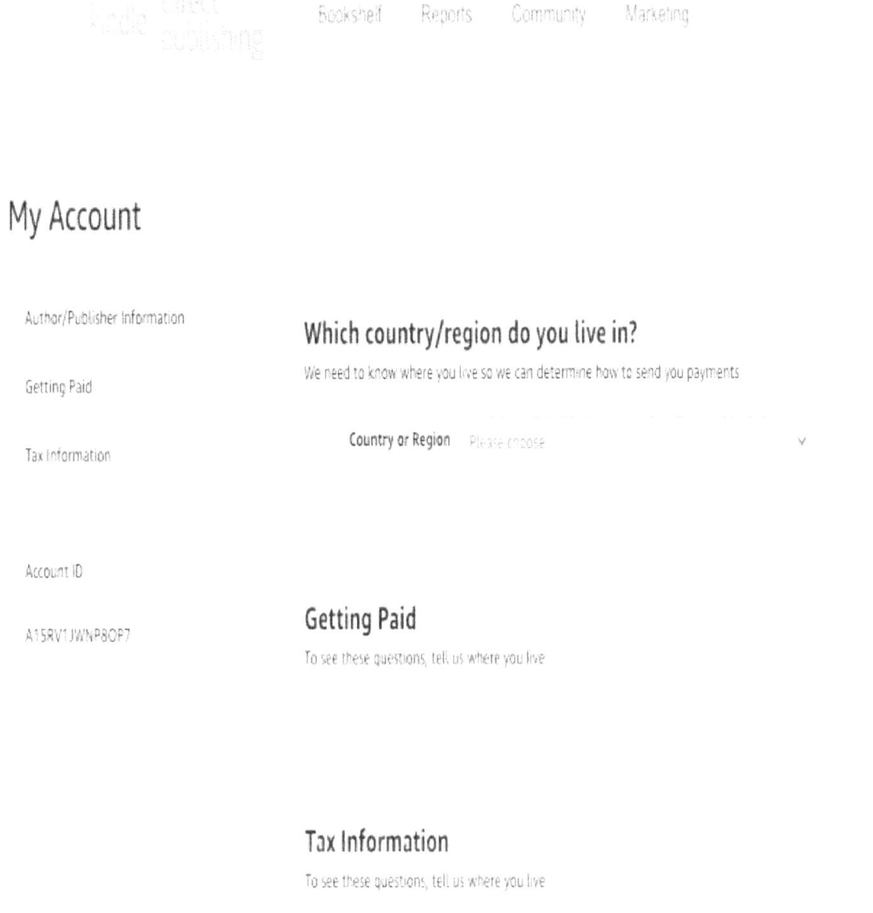

Choose Nigeria by drawing down on the countries or just type N for Nigeria to pop up as a choice
Fill the required field but CLICK: I don't have a bank. Because Nigerian banks do not qualify
If your books are sold, Amazon will mail your checks to you here in Nigeria. Cheque for the UK audience in our group.

This is what you will see and you are almost there.

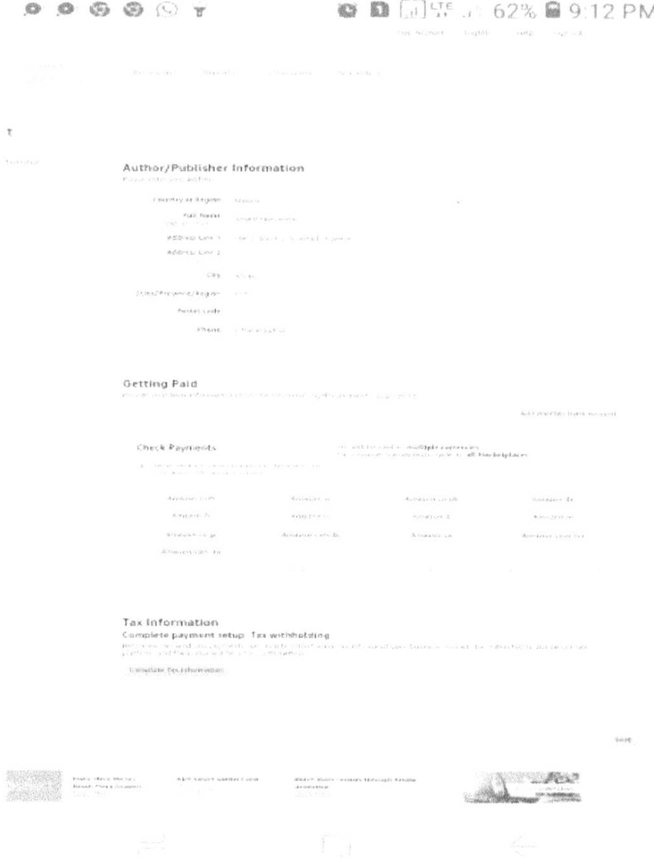

Now let move to the Tax information: Click on the *Save and preview* to actually preview the filled form as below��

On the tax information, if you have TIN issued to you, then input the details, but if not please enter your details as it affect your country.

��, then listen to how to deal with that column effectively in the video below��

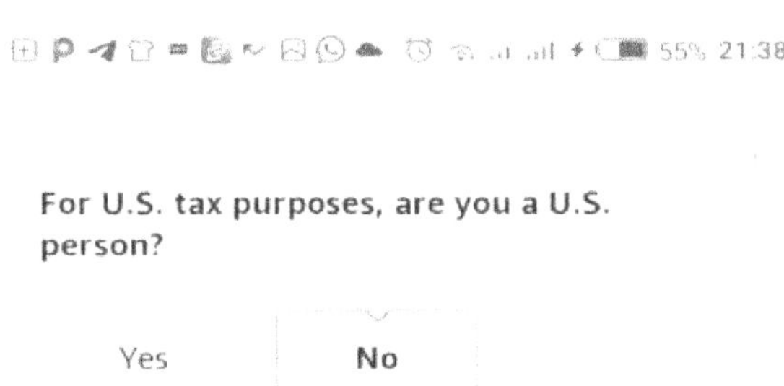

For U.S. tax purposes, are you a U.S. person?

Yes   **No**

Are you acting as an intermediary agent, or other person receiving payment on behalf of another person or as a flow-through entity?

Yes   **No**

Tax Identity Information

Full name

Rosemary Ekemena Arabono

⚠ If no TIN is provided, any reduction of the 30% statutory withholding tax rate applicable to your U.S. source payments will not apply.

Why are you not able to provide a TIN?

◉ The country where I am liable to pay tax does not issue TINs to its residents.

○ I have applied for a TIN but haven't received it yet.

○ I could not/have not obtained TIN from my local authorities because of other reasons.

ⓘ To receive any tax reductions related to your status, you can apply for a US TIN if not already done so. For more information, please visit IRS Instructions

Continue

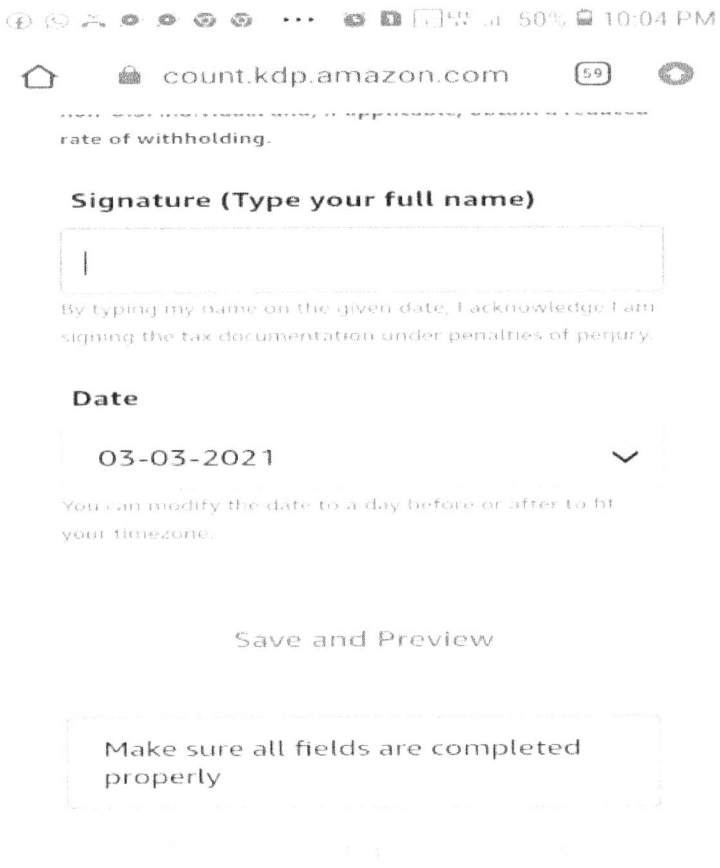

50% 10:04 PM
count.kdp.amazon.com
59
rate of withholding.
Signature (Type your full name)
By typing my name on the given date, I acknowledge I am signing the tax documentation under penalties of perjury.
Date
03-03-2021
You can modify the date to a day before or after to fit your timezone.
Save and Preview
Make sure all fields are completed properly

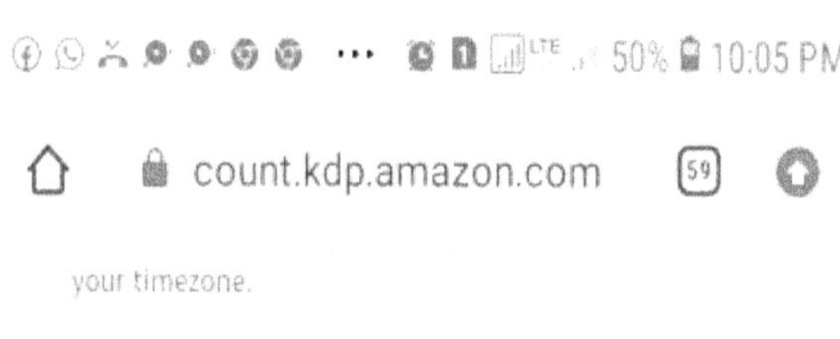
50% 10:05 PM
count.kdp.amazon.com
your timezone.

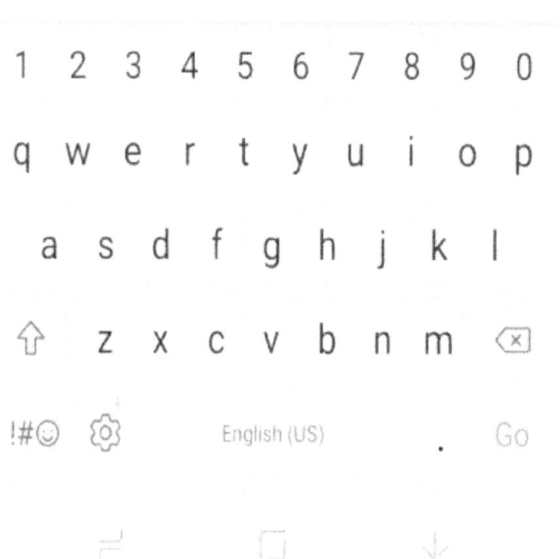
Save and Preview
Exit without saving
© 2013-2021, Amazon.com, Inc. or its affiliates
1 2 3 4 5 6 7 8 9 0
q w e r t y u i o p
a s d f g h j k l
z x c v b n m
!#☺
English (US)
Go

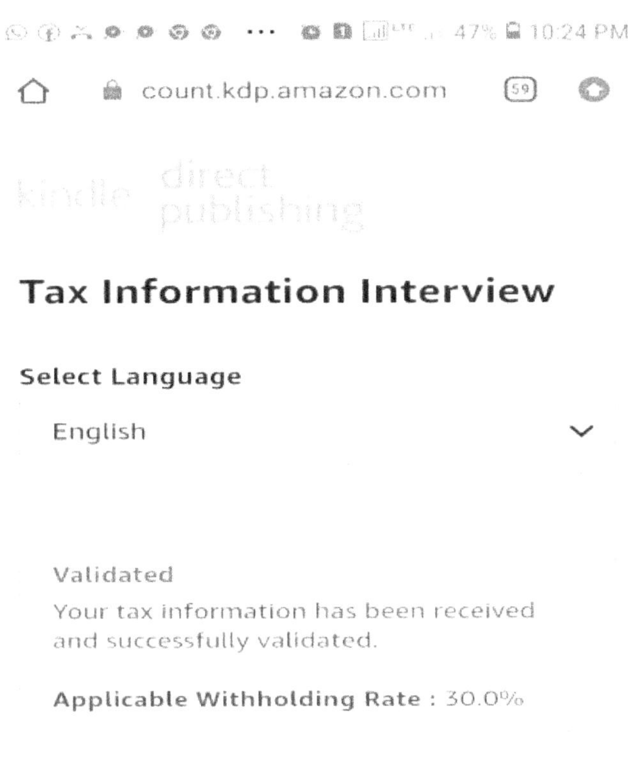

Once all this are done and you are good to go and your account is complete. Below is a picture of how the account look like at the final stage.

count.kdp.amazon.com
My Account
Author/Publisher Information
Getting Paid
Check Payments
Tax Information
Need to update your tax information?

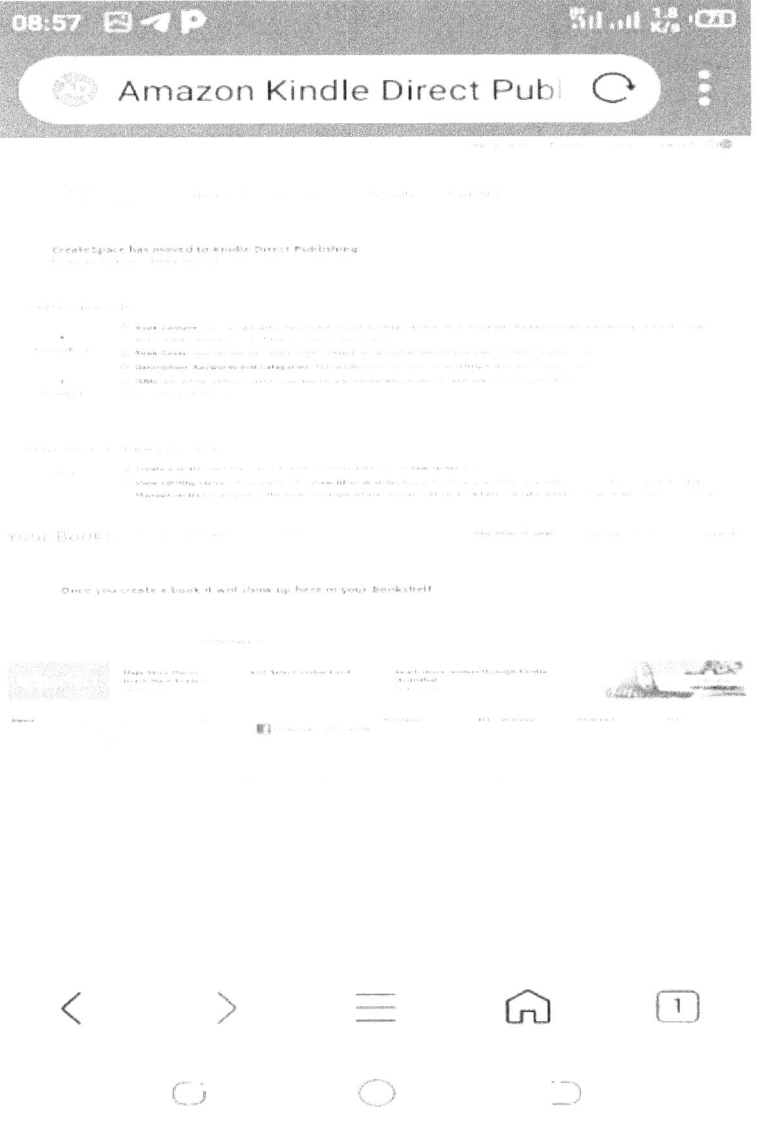

How to Publish and Upload Your eBook: follow the steps below.

1. Sign in into your KDP account through KDP.AMAZON-.COM
2. You will get to your account page. At the top you will find BOOKSHELF click on it
3. Go to the icon CREAT EBOOK.

NB: Ensure your manuscript have been formatted in line with the template that you most have downloaded CREATE-SPACE FORMAT TEMPLETE

4. When you click on the icon CREATE EBOOK it will take you through a three steps seen below
a. You will create your cover page for your eBook. You could pick an image from your gallery and design.
b. Then proceed to content (the size have been updated to be normal)
c. Click on bleeds and upload your manuscript.

CHAPTER SIX

PRACTICAL FOR COVER CREATION USING THE COVER CREATION TOOLS

For Practical Cover Creation Using the Cover Creator Tool You'd need these status

1. Ensure you've published your eBooks to the point of cover creation. So all those who are yet to publish their eBooks should ensure they get there before practical class commences.

2. Authors image must be ready

3. Any image you need for the front cover - this is optional as you can use from the KDP gallery.

We have two types of cover creation, they are eBook cover creation and paperback cover creation.

1. GUIDE TO EBOOK COVER CREATION: The following steps will aid you in creating of your eBook cover page.

    I.   Log on to you page, select the book you want to publish, it will the take you to a three stage form where all the information need for the publication will be required.

II. Click on cover creation then Launch cover

III. Click on the choice of where you want to pick your image from eg. Kindle image gallery for the purpose of this book.

IV. Click the image you want

V. Click on style these will give you different options on what you want to edit eg. colour, font size, layout etc.

VI. Click on preview

VII. Click approve, saved and submit.

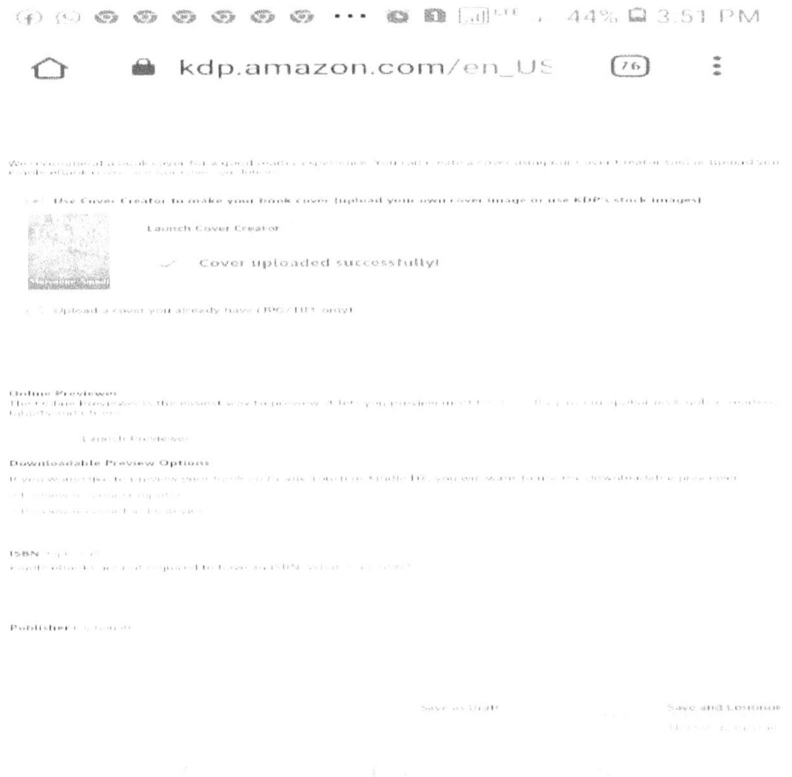

2. GUIDE TO PAPERBACCK COVER CREATION: The following step-by-step will aid you in the creating you paperback cover page for your publication.

    I.   Log on to you page, select the book you want to create the paperback cover

    II.   Click on cover creation

    III.   Click Launch cover creation, the a three stage form to fill will pop up

    IV.   Pick your choice of front cover image

    V.   Click on style this will give you option to edit things like colour, font size, name etc.

    VI.   Click on author it will take you to your computer and choose the picture you want to use and save the picture

    VII.   Click preview and Click save and submit

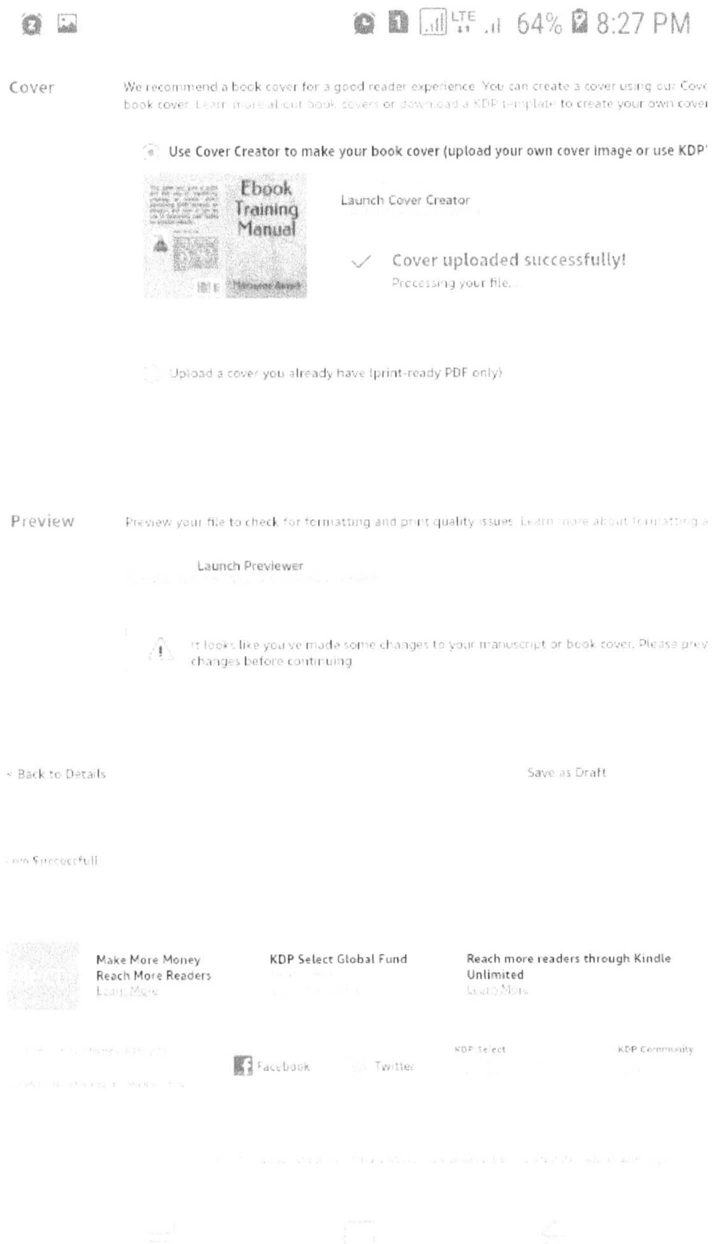

PAPERBACK CONTENT EDITING

Click on design

Click on where you want to the author biography and edit

Click on the summary and edit
Click on save and submit

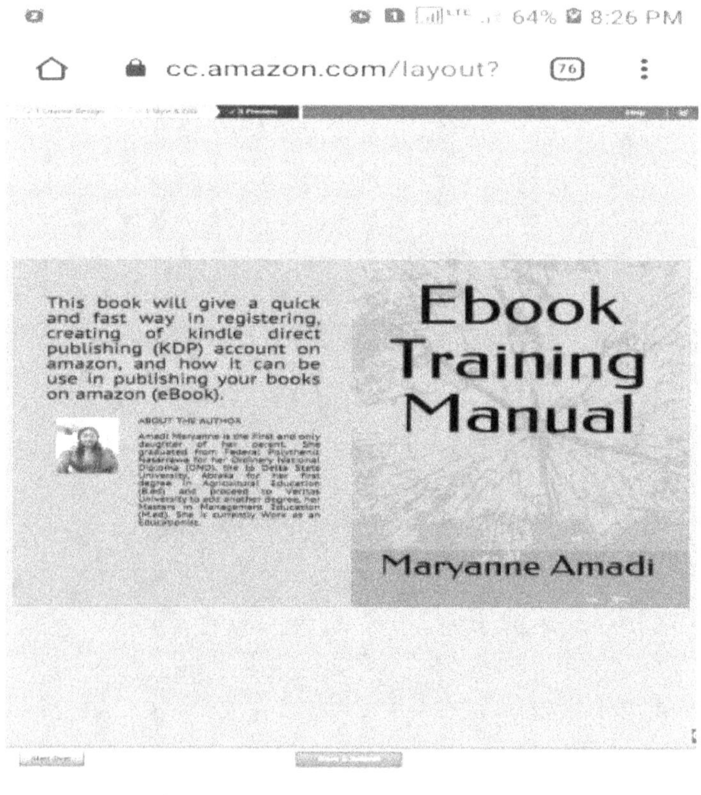

CHAPTER SEVEN

ALL ABOUT KINDLE CREATE APPLICATION

Downloading of the Kindle Create Application is what you will see in this chapter and is the main purpose of the book. With the steps below all you need to know will be achieved.

How To Download Kindle Create Application

You can download kindle create app with these following steps

1. Log on to your account
2. Screw down to get started and click. It will take you to kindle tool and resource, the first thing you will see is a heading ''manuscript formatting''.
3. Screw to under the image and click kindle create, it will take you to the amazon home page
4. Click on download (it could be on a computer or mac book), in this case you click on download for PC
5. When you are done downloading, then you will have to install the app and finally the app is ready for use.

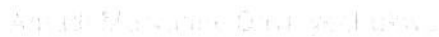

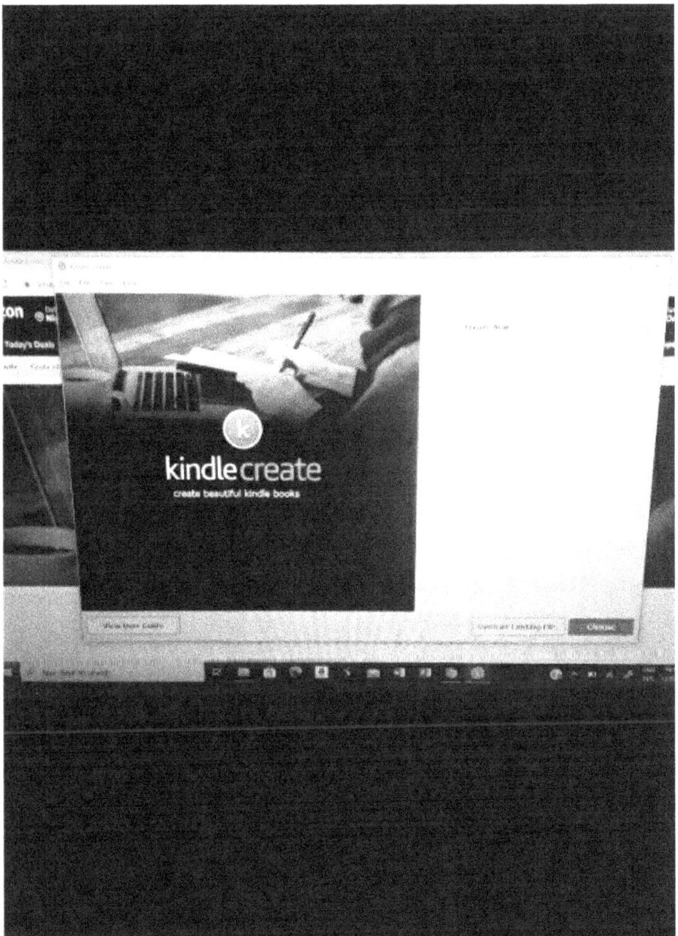
kindlecreate
create beautiful kindle books

CHAPTER EIGHT

NAVIGATING THROUGH THE KINDLE CREATE APPLICATION (THE ADVANCE METHOD)

The use of the kindle create application in uploading and formatting of your books for publication can be done in the step-by-step process below:

1. Open your kindle create app.
2. Click on choose this is because it is your first time using the app as no previous book has been formatted with the app.
3. Click on choose the file in other for you to pick from your computer the book that you want to format.
4. Click on continue when the file has import successfully
5. The click start and your book will be formatted for you, it may take a little time (when you click the start it will suggest a table of content for you and you can decides to either used it of make your own from the front matter).

Note: every book has something to say, and so at the left top of the page you will see a bar called

1. Front Matter it has to do with title page, copyright, introduction, dedication table of content and the likes. All you have to do is click on the any one you want to input in the book when it show fill and save. Click on insert table of content to insert it,
2. Body it has to do with the content of the book that you want to publish.
3. Back Matter it has to do with the about the author, praise for the author, acknowledgements, afterword and the likes. All you have to do is click on the any one you want to input in the book when it show fill and save.

On the right bar you will see things such as:

1. Theme which gives you the options of how you want the book to appear
2. Print setting which gives you the options of how you want the book to appear that is the interior
3. Preview here you have to change to go through your work to be sure if it ok for publication
4. Publish when you click it your work will be save as a kdf file and it will replace the unformatted file.

The steps are shown with pictures below:

kindle create
create beautiful kindle books

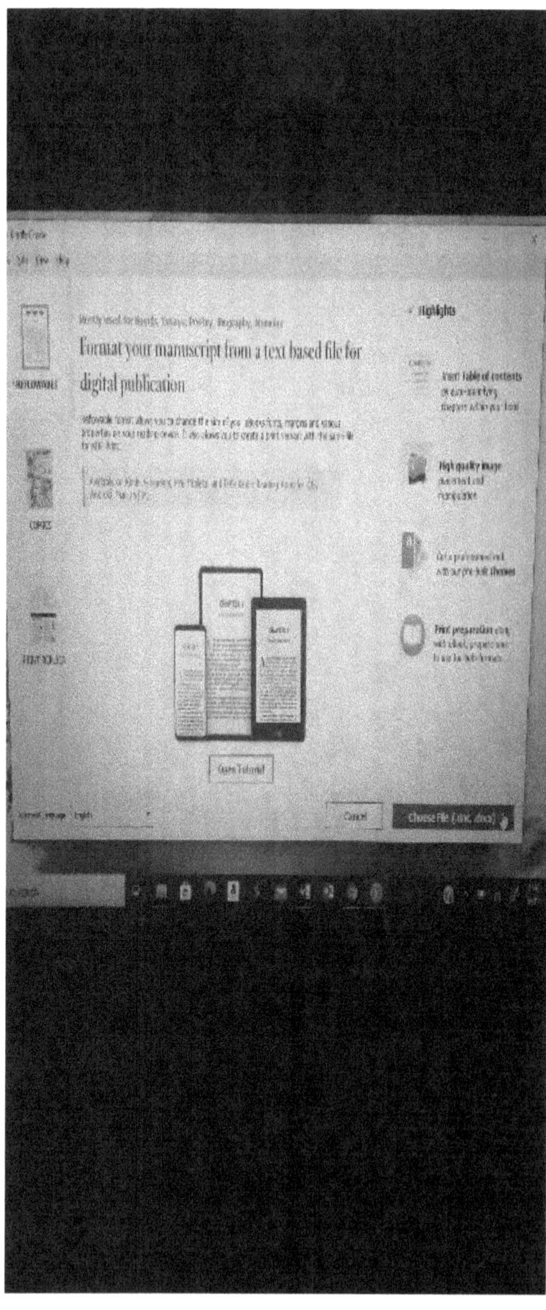

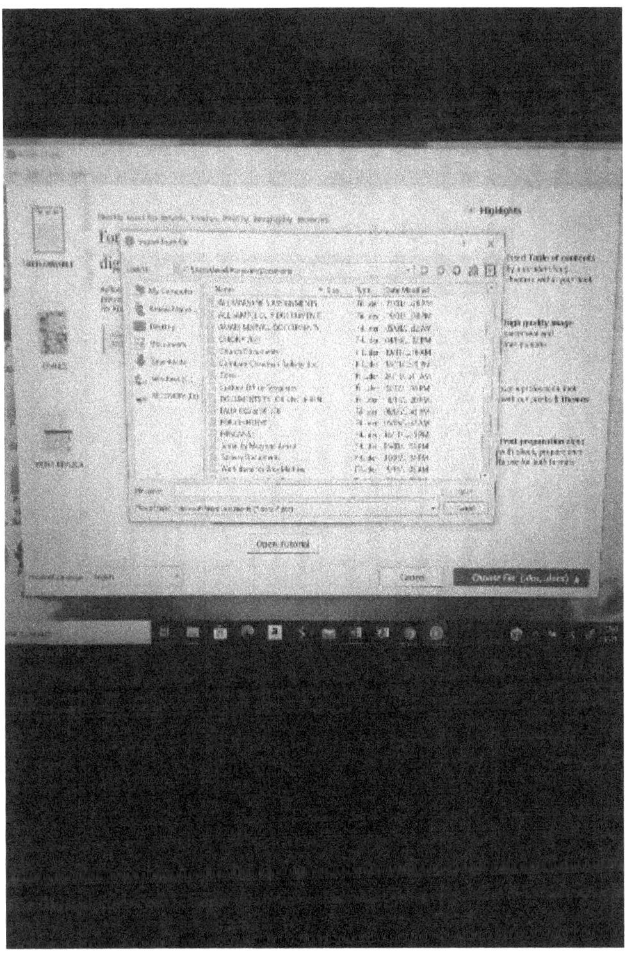

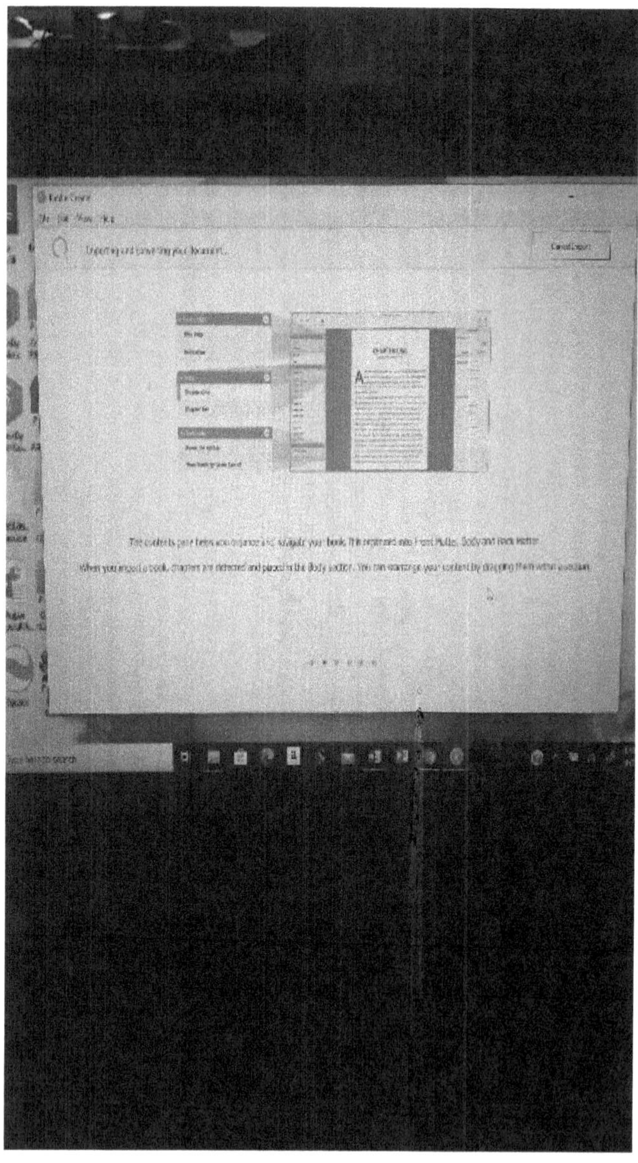

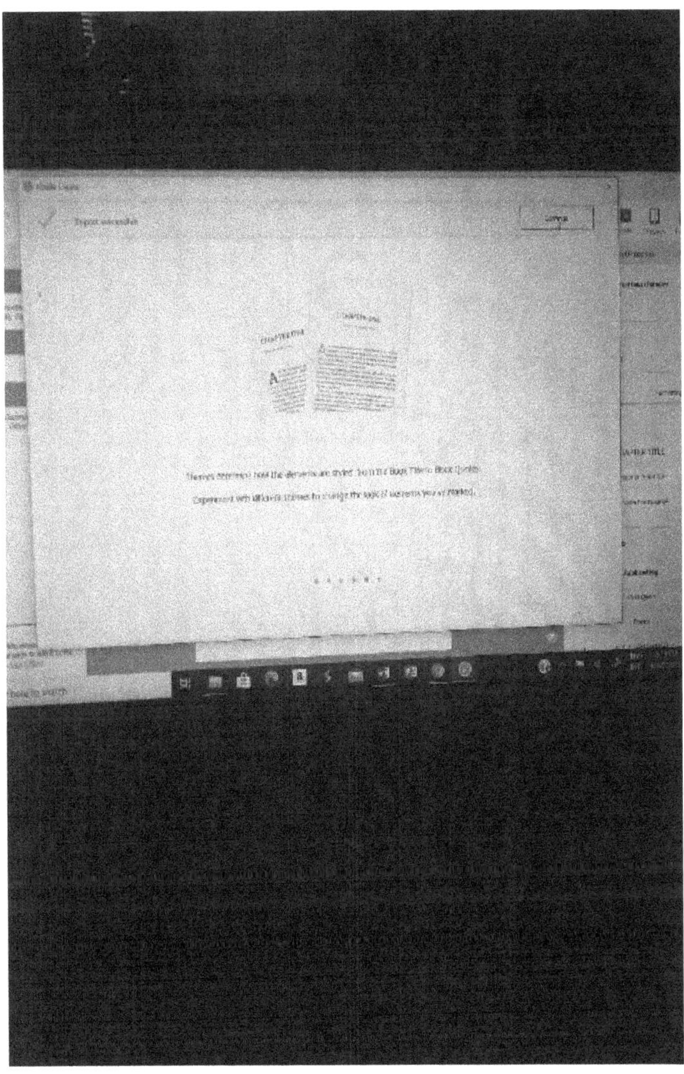

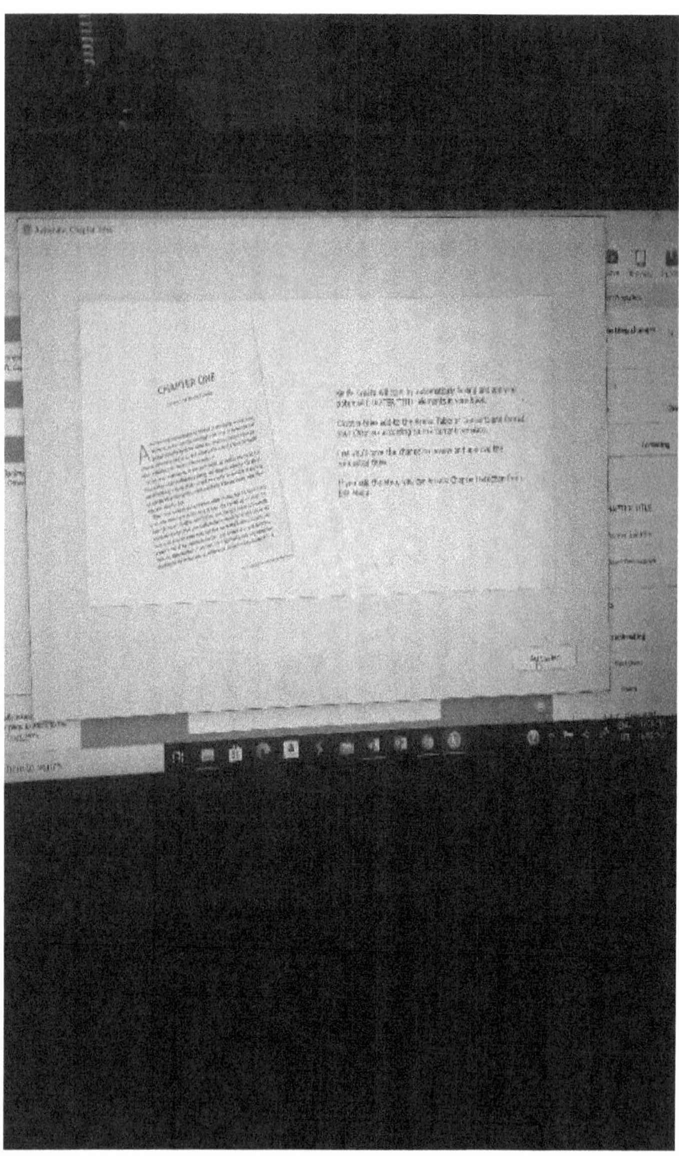

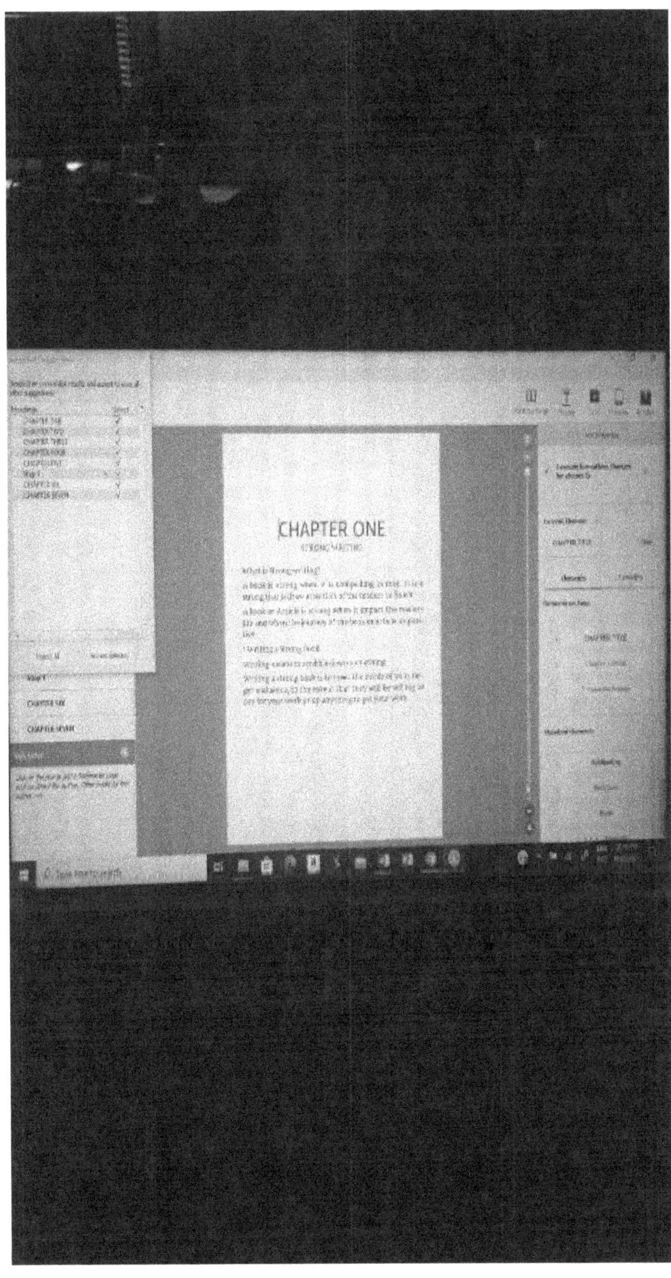

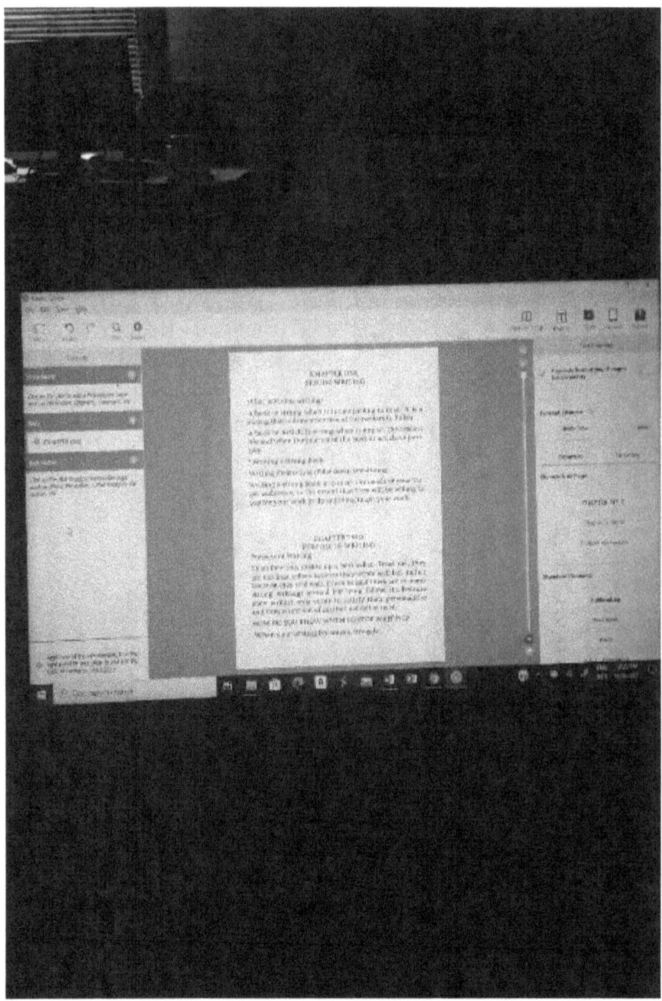

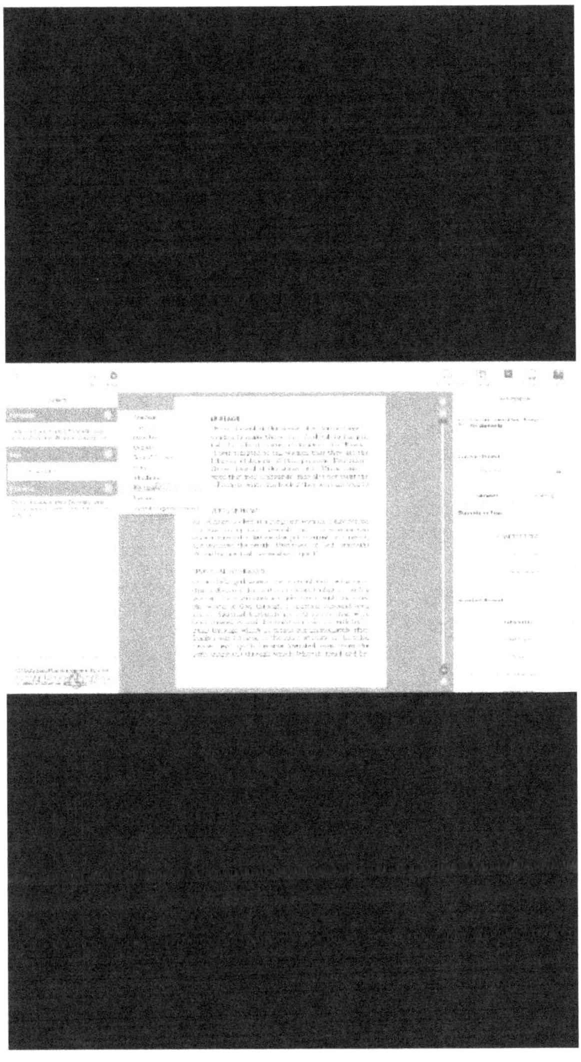

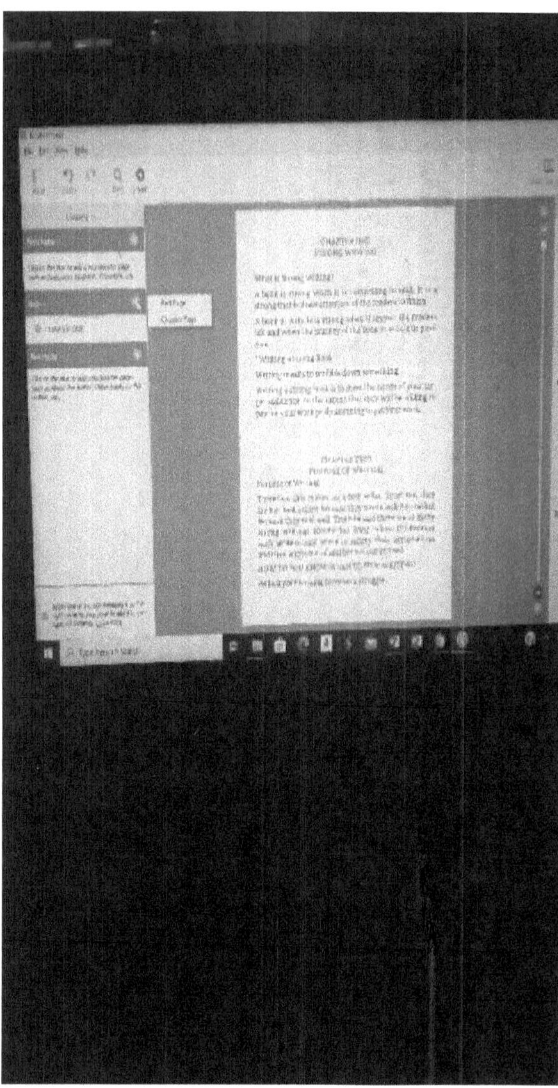

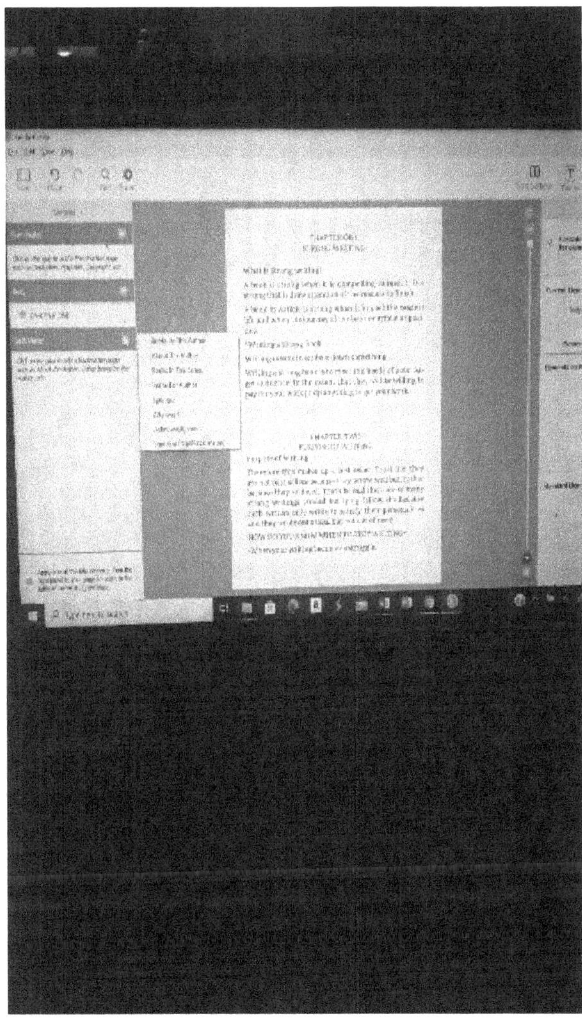

CHAPTER NINE

HOW TO GET FREE ISBN FROM KDP

To get a free ISBN fron KDP is very possible and easy with the following steps.

1. Log on to your KDP account
2. Click on bookshelf
3. Click on publish paper back
4. Fill the three stage form that will appear,
5. On the second stage of the form you will see assign me a free KDP ISBN
6. An ISBN will be assign to you and with this you have your ISBN for the book you want to publish. This can be seen the picture below.

78% 9:34 PM
Lite   kdp.amazon.com/   78
ng Manual
ils   Paperback Content   Paperback Rights & Pricir
             In Progress   Not Started
To comply with industry standards, all paperbacks are required to have a unique ISBN. What is an ISBN?
Get a free KDP ISBN
Assign me a free KDP ISBN   Your book has been assigned a free KDP ISBN
                                   ISBN: 9798722230348
                                   Imprint: Independently published
Use my own ISBN
Enter the date on which your book was first published. Leave this blank if you are publishing your book for the first time.
my book's publication date determined?
Publication Date (Optional)
Your "Live on Amazon" date will be used
The default options selected below are based on the most common selections. How will printing cost be calculated?
Interior & paper type
What ink and paper types does KDP support?
Black & white interior   Black & white interior   Premium color interior
with cream paper   with white paper   with white paper
Trim Size
What is a trim size?
6 x 9 in   Select a different size
15.24 x 22.86 cm
Bleed Settings

ACKNOWLEDGEMENT

My immensurable gratitude goes to God, the Almighty who generously gave me the strength, endurance and resource to write this book to complete. I wish to specially thank my parents, brothers, sisters in laws, nieces. I can't forget to thank Rev. Sr. Rosemary, Mrs. Okpa and of cause Mr. Solomon who took out time to train me to be successful. Finally to my friend and family. Thank to you all. My immensurable gratitude goes to God, the Almighty who generously gave me the strength, endurance and resource to write this book to complete. I wish to specially thank my parents, brothers, sisters in laws, nieces. I can't forget to thank Rev. Sr. Rosemary, Mrs. Okpa and of cause Mr. Solomon who took out time to train me to be successful. Finally to my friend and family. Thank to you all.

ABOUT THE AUTHOR

Maryanne Amadi

Amadi Maryanne is the First and only daughter of her parent. She graduated from Federal Polytechnic Nasarrawa for her Ordinary National Diploma (OND), then to Delta State University, Abraka for her first degree in Agricultural Education (B.ed) and proceed to Veritas University to add another degree, her Masters in Management Education (M.ed). She is educationist and currently working with Duliz Dredging and Construction Nigeria Limited as the administration officer.